The Family Table

a journal for recipes and memories

Georgeanne Brennan

Em oi

Doi khong co em

Nhu pho

Kong co nuoc leo

Oh my beloved,
life without you
is like
Pho without its broth
~*Vietnamese saying*

CHRONICLE BOOKS

SAN FRANCISCO

D1411049

Page 158 constitutes a continuation of the copyright page.

Text by Georgeanne Brennan
Illustrations by Elvis Swift
Photography research by Julie Glantz
Design by Gayle Steinbeigle
Printed in Hong Kong
Typeset in Futura and Mrs. Eaves

ISBN 0-8118-2412-8

10 9 8 7 6 5 4 3 2 1

Distributed in Canada by
Raincoast Books
8680 Cambie Street
Vancouver, B.C. V6P 6M9

Chronicle Books
85 Second Street
San Francisco, CA 94105
www.chroniclebooks.com

Food is one of the great commonalities of our lives, reaching across barriers of age, time, place, language, and customs—linking us to each other, to those who have gone before us, and to those who are yet to come. Sitting around a table sharing food with family, friends, acquaintances, or strangers draws us together with a common purpose. But more than just eating occurs around the table. We talk, discuss, argue, remain silent, fiddle our hands, laugh, pout, and act on our best behavior—or occasionally our worst.

The preparation, cooking, and sharing of food is one of our most meaningful connections with each other. Since eating is a necessity, food is something that we all have in common. When we prepare food and share meals—whether at home, at family gatherings, or far away—all of our senses are engaged. The appearance of food and its tastes, textures, and aromas draw us into a relationship with a particular place and moment. Food memories are emotional and sensory triggers for the larger scope of time, circumstance, and the recollection of things past.

Food brings forth memories. Some are of sparse fare, some of feasts and celebrations, some belong to our childhood, and others to our adult lives. Writing about our family table—whether a table for two, for a dozen, for an extended family, or a friend's table—allows us to *fix our feelings and experiences in time as we explore our family's personal memories and find the stories that lie behind a particular dish or food experience.*

This book provides a place to write down those memories by person- ally reminiscing, by questioning family members and noting their recollections, and by collecting recipes. Exploring family memories through the medium of food offers a means of discovering and remembering your family's history—as well as how it helped make you who you are.

I once asked a friend about his strongest memory of food. He told me that it was the stories his parents had told about being hungry in Germany during the war years. He had been a child of the 1960s and had never gone hungry. His family's cupboards, refrigerator, and freezer were filled with food—peanut butter, chocolate ice cream, oatmeal, Rice Krispies, bacon, eggs, lima beans, tuna. His mother cooked a sit-down dinner every night, and dessert was almost always a home-baked sweet. But in his mind's eye he saw the hard, half-loaf of bread in the dimly lit kitchen in a small town in the Rhineland, and the knobby carrots surreptitiously dug from a neighbor's garden. In his stomach he could feel the tight fist of hunger when the bread and carrots were gone, and there was no more to eat. When he asked his parents about what they ate, he learned about the windows broken at their favorite candy shop because the owner was Jewish; about how the family's table was always set with a cloth, even when there was nothing but bread to eat; and about the cousins who used to visit often...then never came again.

Remembering a certain food or dish evokes a memory not only of its taste, but of the context in which it was eaten. For me, the taste of apple pie still warm from the oven, fragrant with the scent of cinna- mon, conjures up a memory of my Aunt Louise's kitchen where I used to sit and eat her pie. There is the screen door framed in green wood

that she asked us not to slam as we came running into the kitchen, our faces flushed from playing on the creaking swing set. The remembered feel of the apple pie, firm and soft on the tongue, projects an image of the mottled plastic and chrome table and chairs in the middle of the room, the cream-colored, ruffled curtains on the windows that Aunt Louise kept starched and pressed. The smell of her Texas kitchen, her hands still dusty with flour, the stray curl that was perpetually in her eye as she cooked, and how small she seemed in the hospital bed the last time I saw her—all these memories come rushing in with the taste of warm apples.

I can never eat ripe California olives, their pits replaced by perfectly round holes, without thinking of my father. Every Thanksgiving my brother and I would sneak a handful of olives from the relish tray, fit an olive on each finger, then greedily eat them one by one from our finger-tips before our father caught us. When he did, he always laughed, saying he was going to eat them first. On the first Thanksgiving after our father died, when my brother was thirteen, we put the olives on our fingers as usual to try to make the holiday seem normal, but it didn't work.

This book is meant to be not only a journal, but a book that when completed will serve as a record of your own family's food history, to be shared with your family and with coming generations. Recollections of brothers and sisters, mothers, fathers, aunts, uncles, grandparents, and great-grandparents each have a place. Recipes are an important part of these recollections. Most of us have a family member whose reputation for unsurpassed pumpkin pie, latkes, egg rolls, or butter-milk biscuits is legendary. Although you may never really get the secret of Aunt Julia's biscuits, writing the recipe down in her words will allow it to be shared, if not replicated.

The journal is divided into six sections: "Childhood Foods," "Everyday Dishes," "Holidays and Celebrations," "Special Moments," "Away from Home," and "Family Origins." They are followed by a suggested reading list of memoirs and stories related to food and family. Interspersed throughout are quotes from various pieces of literature, such as John Keats' Eve of St. Agnes, Robert Louis Stevenson's Treasure Island, and J.M. Coetzee's Life and Times of Michael K, that speak about the meaning and context of food. Some quotes are about the source of food, such as gardening, hunting, or shopping. Others are about memories of food and the feelings those memories bring. Still others are about a particular meal or a place where a meal was eaten. They are meant to inspire you to write about your own experiences and feelings in the context of food.

This book can be used as a starting point for learning about your family. Sometimes, when asking parents, grandparents, or other relatives where they lived, what they did, and what was important to them, it seems difficult to draw out the detailed information that makes the past, and its people and places, come alive. Many family traditions reside in special recipes, meals, and foods. By focusing on food, many things are discovered not only about the food, but also about the life and times.

For example, "Grandma, what was it like when you and Grandpa first got married?" is such a general question that it might be difficult to put into words the myriad events, feelings, and experiences that make up "first got married." However, "What was the first thing you cooked for Grandpa after you got married?" is a different question, one that allows for a pinpointed response about a particular moment in time. If she says, "Oh, it was ham," you might reply, "Was it a special occasion?"

"No, but it was a Sunday and my mother had always cooked a midday meal on Sunday, often ham, so I thought I should."

"Was it good?"

"Oh, I didn't really know how long to cook it. I stuck it all over with cloves and used toothpicks to spear slices of pineapple to it, like I remember my mother doing."

*From there the conversation might go in a number of different directions—
what was the kitchen like, was there a refrigerator, where did grandpa
work—and with each response comes more questions, leading down paths
filled with details of your family's history.*

Use this book to record family dishes and the stories connected to them.
For example, you could note the year that the family's traditional Thanksgiving
pumpkin pie (and the year that Mom used two tablespoons of ginger
instead of two tablespoons of cinnamon), or the time your sister made
"a special smoothie" for you and it turned out to be a concoction of
dish soap, ice cream, and chocolate syrup. Every family is full of stories.

Be creative in your search for material. Attach photos next to the stories
or recipes. Search through your grandmother's cookbooks for handwrit-
ten notes. Take this journal to Thanksgiving Dinner or a family reunion,
and have each person write in a food memory or favorite dish. Sit down
with your siblings and recreate a typical meal from your teenage years—
perhaps served on mom's second-best china—and record the stories that
emerge. Have your teenagers make a list of their favorite meals and
make copies of your recipes for each of them, so that when they go off to
college they'll be able to recreate a favorite home-cooked meal.

To record family recipes so that others can use them successfully, try
writing the ingredients down in the order in which they are used. If
the person giving you the recipe is vague ("Oh, just take a little flour
and water..."), try to get them to show you about how much, then
translate that into a standard measurement.

At the beginning of the recipe, describe the particular characteristics
or appearance of the dish, because this will help to guide someone
in preparing it. In writing the instructions, be as clear as possible,
giving complete step-by-step instructions. For example, if Aunt Mary
says, "Whip the potatoes," ask her what she uses for whipping—an
electric beater, whisk, hand beater, fork? Sometimes the key to the

particular taste or texture of a beloved dish will lie in some personal aspect of its preparation, not just in its ingredients.

In the instructions, indicate both preparation time and the appearance of the completed dish. For example, "Bake the rhubarb crumble at 375°F for 45 minutes until topping is golden brown, the fruit is soft when poked with a fork, and the juices bubble up around the sides of the dish." This kind of information gives the cook a great deal of help, especially if preparing an unfamiliar dish. The recipe itself can be written in a number of different formats. It can be written entirely in prose, including the ingredient measurements: "Take a 3½ pound chicken and rub it thoroughly, inside and out, with 1 tablespoon of paprika, ½ teaspoon of pepper, and ½ teaspoon of freshly ground pepper. Fill the cavity with several 4 to 5-inch lengths of fresh thyme. Roast it uncovered at 350°F for an hour and 15 minutes, or until the skin is crisp and golden brown. Remove and let it stand for 10 to 15 minutes before carving." The same recipe can be written with a list of ingredients and the steps numbered, or written in paragraph form. More important than the style you choose is the clarity of description and the inclusion of all the necessary steps.

As you use this book to record the stories and history of your family table, you will discover the ways it works best for you—as a journal of personal food memories, as a collection of family recipes, as a series of family recollections about time and place, or perhaps all three. You may want to prepare several books, one for yourself and copies to give to family members. You will no doubt discover that you are developing your own family food traditions, as well as passing on those of previous generations.

Peanut butter and jelly sandwiches on white bread, Jell-O cubes, tapioca pudding, plain rice with soy sauce, split pea soup, mustard and onion sandwiches, Hostess cherry pies, Lipton's noodle soup, chocolate pies, baked potato with sour cream and chives—we all have a list of favorite dishes that hold memories of time and place.

If a favorite food (say bread-and-butter pickles) brings to mind your grandmother's refrigerator where she always kept an open jar of homemade bread-and-butter pickles, include that in your list, with perhaps a description of her kitchen or of a visit when you ate the pickles.

My own grandmother taught me to make onion and mustard sandwiches. I would often go to stay with her in her little duplex in El Monte, California. We'd sew, cook, and garden together, and during the day we'd have snacks. A small woman with pure white hair cut short, she would take a piece of bread (any kind) and spread it with mustard. Then she'd thinly slice an onion—red are best, she told me, because they are sweeter—and lay the slices on the bread, open-face style. Then we would sit together and share the sandwiches.

I shall remember always the mysterious, beautiful sensation of well-being I felt, when I was small, to hear my mother talk of the suppers she used to eat at boarding school. They were called "midnight feasts," and were kept secret, supposedly, from the teachers, in the best tradition of the 1890s. They consisted of oyster loaf. There may have been other things. Maybe the most daring young ladies even drank ginger beer, although I am afraid it was more likely sweet raspberry shrub or some such unfortunate potation. Maybe there were cigarettes, and pickles, and bonbons. But it is the oyster loaf that I remember.

Consider the Oyster, M. F. K. Fisher

My favorite
sandwich is
peanut butter,
baloney, cheddar
cheese, lettuce,
and mayonnaise
on toasted bread
with catsup on
the side.

~ Hubert Humphrey, 1966

A basin of nice
smooth gruel, thin,
but not too thin.

~ *Emma*, Jane Austen

What is patriotism
but the love of good
things we ate in
our childhood?

~ Lin Yutang, 1935

With her first bite of crayfish
etouffèe, Sidda could see her mother
in the kitchen at Pecan Grove. She saw Vivi
first melting butter in a large cast-iron skillet,
then slowly stirring flour into the butter, and
cooking the roux until it became a chestnut brown.
She smelled the onions, celery, and green peppers as
Vivi added them to the roux. She saw the dish change
color as Vivi added the crayfish tails, along with fresh
parsley, cayenne pepper, and generous shakes of the
ever-present Tabasco bottle. With each bite, Sidda
tasted her homeland and her mother's love.

—— *Divine Secrets of the Ya-Ya Sisterhood*, Rebecca Wells

When God
gives hard bread
He gives sharp teeth.

~ German Proverb

Many's the long
night I've dreamed of
cheese—toasted mostly.

~ Ben Gunn in *Treasure Island*,
Robert Louis Stevenson

Everyday food varies at different times in our lives, according to background and circumstances. Remember cafeteria food in school with its cyclical rounds of beef casseroles, chicken and noodles, macaroni and cheese, meatloaf, and the occasional tamale pie, fried chicken, and pepper steak? Or the early married days with a growing family when tuna noodle casserole, red beans and rice, melted cheese sandwiches, fish sticks, and other budget stretchers appeared more often than not, and when dessert was Jell-O or pudding?

These remembered, everyday dishes conjure up memories of a shared event or personal feelings, and here is the place to tell the tale. Maybe it was the first time your little brother ever ate solid food, and he slammed his little spoon with delight, spewing macaroni and cheese in every direction, or the fruit salad made with peaches and nectarines you had picked yourself with a friend while visiting a farm.

Chopped iceberg lettuce, two or three slices of a tomato, and a dollop of bottled blue cheese dressing served in an individual wooden bowl—a salad we had every night for dinner—never fail to bring to my mind's eye the picture of my mother bustling around in our peach-colored kitchen with scalloped wooden valences painted pale turquoise. The memory of how intensely my mother wanted those colors, and how agreeable my father was to it rapidly follows, as does my feeling of mortification at having what I considered to be such an outlandish color combination when everyone else I knew had a white or a yellow kitchen with suitable trim.

...And Chin, too, thought how nice that would be. An egg, fried and then chopped into little pieces with perhaps some bits of mushroom. A little garlic for flavor and for health. Bread to fill the stomach. He had gotten quite used to bread. Lair led them past the stairs and into the kitchen. It was a small room. A rough wooden table and six chairs filled it.

Sarah Canary, Karen Joy Fowler

...A hungry man
can do no deep study,
    and thus must God,
   through such default,
    lose the best prayers.

~ *The Flowering Light of God*,
Mechtild von Magdeburg

How beautiful
and strong those
buttered onions come
to my nose!

~ *Letter to Thomas Manning*,
Charles Lamb

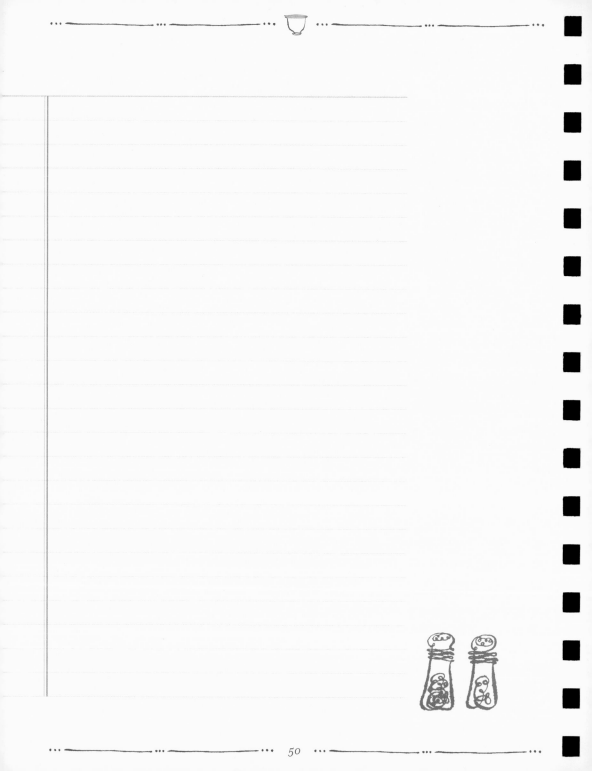

If the people
have no bread
let them eat cake.

~ attributed to
Marie Antoinette, 1789

Holiday meals and settings define our family heritage and traditions. Many holidays have their roots in religious ceremonies and celebrations, such as Hanukkah, Easter, Christmas, Purim, and All Saints Day. Others are celebrations of national independence, of seasonal change, and of personal events—birthdays, weddings, graduations, family reunions.

Our grandparents, great-grandparents, and those before them brought their family traditions to this country when they came as immigrants; they have passed this heritage down to us through special dishes and foods prepared and eaten only during certain times of the year.

Once here, other traditions developed as well. Father's Day is celebrated with a manly brunch, perhaps of scrambled eggs, smoked salmon, and heaps of toast and homemade jam, and Labor Day with picnics of hot dogs, hamburgers, and chocolate cake.

Food is part of these traditions. This chapter is a good place to record special recipes, along with the anecdotes and family rituals that lie behind them and stories about particular holidays.

"A loaf of bread," the Walrus said,

"Is what we chiefly need:

Pepper and vinegar besides

Are very good indeed—

Now if you're ready Oysters, dear,

We can begin to feed!"

Through the Looking Glass, Lewis Carroll

An egg is dear
on Easter Day.

~ Anonymous

There is no one who
became rich because he
broke a holiday, and not one
who became fat because he
broke a fast.

~ Ethiopian Proverb

Let me see; what am I to buy for
our sheep-shearing feast? Three pound
of sugar, five pound of currants, rice,—
what will this sister of mine do with rice...
I must have saffron to colour the warden pies;
mace, dates?—none, that's out of my note; nutmegs,
seven; a race or two of ginger, but that I may beg; four
pound of prunes, and as many of raisins o' the sun.

The Winter's Tale, William Shakespeare

Strange to see
how a good dinner
and feasting reconciles
everybody.

~ *Diary*, Samuel Pepys

A smell like an
eating-house and a
pastrycook's next door
to each other, with a
laundry next door
to that. That was
the pudding.

~ *A Christmas Carol*,
Charles Dickens

I remember the first time I went out to an "adult" restaurant with friends and without my parents or other adults. Three of us went to a French restaurant and because we were in our second year of high school French, felt very knowledgeable about ordering. A white-aproned waiter took our request for onion soup, coq au vin, and chocolate mousse. I have never felt more grown-up, more sure that life was going to be a wonderful adventure than I did that early winter evening sitting at our candlelit table, talking about how much we loved Le Petit Prince *and what it would be like when we went to Paris someday and walked the streets and neighborhoods where Degas and Modigliani painted.*

A special occasion might be the time you shared an egg salad sandwich with the sixth grade boy you had a crush on, or the delight in your grandmother's eye when she saw that you had remembered her favorite chocolates, even though she was too ill to eat them.

It might be a special occasion recounted by another family member, such as the time your great-grandmother caught her first fish and cooked it over an open campfire, or the time your father took your mother to a Hollywood diner on their first date and each pretended to see a movie star, or the first meal your mother cooked for her in-laws, when she didn't realize she had to thaw the turkey first before she cooked it.

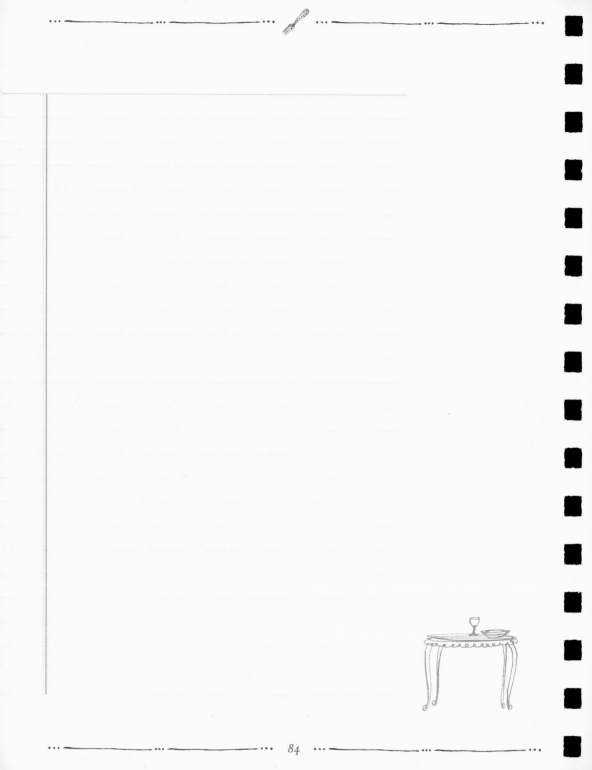

My dinner was brought, and Four Persons of Quality, whom I remember to have seen very near the King's Person, did me the honour to dine with me. We had two Courses, of three Dishes each. In the first Course, there was a Shoulder of Mutton cut into an Aequilateral Triangle, a piece of Beef into a Rhomboides, and a Pudding into a Cycloid. The second Course was two ducks trussed up into the Form of Fiddles; Sausages and Puddings resembling flutes and Haut-boys, and a Breast of Veal in the shape of a Harp. The Servants cut out Bread into Cones, Cylinders, Parallelograms, and several other Mathematical Figures.

Gulliver's Travels, Jonathan Swift

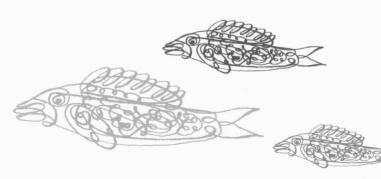

Everything ends this
way in France—everything:
weddings, christenings, duels,
burials, swindlings, diplomatic
affairs—everything is a pretext
for a good dinner.

~ *Cecile*, Jean Anouilh

And still she slept an azure-lidded sleep,

In blanched linens, smooth, and lavender'd

While he from forth the closet brought a heap

of candied apple, quince, and plum, and gourd;

With jellies soother than the creamy curd,

And lucent syrops, tinct with cinnamon;

Manna and dates, in argosy transferr'd

From Fez; and spiced dainties, every one,

From silken Samarcand to cedar'd Lebanon.

~ *The Eve of St. Agnes*, John Keats

He assembled his relatives to the number of forty, at a feast served in the court of his house, as was the usage of grand councils which precede great revolutions among the Arabs. They were all the sons and descendents of his uncle and adoptive father, Aboutaleb. The banquet, frugal, like the life of the desert, was composed of but a leg of mutton and some rice. Mahomet supplied its meagerness by the nutrient of the soul; he entertained his guests with so much inspiration and persuasion that they felt themselves satisfied by his words.

Lamartine's *Turkey*

My wife had got
ready a very fine
dinner—*viz*, a dish of
marrow bone; a leg of mutton;
a loin of veal, a dish of fowl;
three pullets and two dozen of
larks all in a dish; a great tart,
a neat's tongue, a dish of
anchovies, a dish of prawns
and cheese.

~ *Diary*, Samuel Pepys

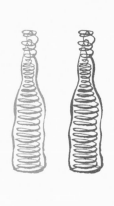

They had gone to a big
restaurant with white table
linens and waiters in dinner coats,
as though there had never been a
war at all. For an enormous price
they had eaten roast chicken and fried
potatoes and pastries, and they had
had champagne all right, champagne
which the Germans had brought to
Rome from France.

~ *The Man in the Grey Flannel Suit*,
 Sloan Wilson

Away from home has many meanings. It can be the adventure of food discovered and eaten in an unfamiliar place while traveling, or it can be the loss of familiar food due to war, poverty, or change. It encompasses the exhilarating experience of being someplace new, eating a new food such as sushi or chicken mole for the first time, or the daunting and embarrassing experience of being served unfamiliar food—such as crayfish still in their shells or banana leaf tamales—and not knowing how to eat it.

You can use this section to recall the time you had a picnic on a hillside in Tuscany with a bottle of red wine, rounds of soft cheeses, and sweet, ripe fruit, remembering the way the wind moved softly among the olive trees below. A wonderful restaurant meal could be described here, or the homesickness you felt when you were ill at camp and instead of the special honey-lemon tea your mother gave you, you got only a spoonful of bright green medicine.

I remember being invited by a French neighbor to her home for dinner. I was horrified when confronted by blood sausages, the meal's main course. However, I was even more mortified at the thought of refusing the food and insulting the neighbor who had befriended me in the small French village where I was living. So I ate the blood sausage, along with the mashed potatoes and apples she served; it was delicious, and I eventually learned how to make my own.

The mistake I made, he thought, going back in time, was not to have had plenty of seeds, a different packet of seeds for each pocket: pumpkin seeds, marrow seeds, beans, carrot seeds, beet-root seeds, onion seeds, tomato seeds, spinach seeds. Seeds in my shoes too, and in the lining of my coat, in case of robbers along the way. Then my mistake was to plant all my seeds together in one patch. I should have planted them one at a time spread out over miles of veldt in patches of soil no larger than my hand, and drawn a map and kept it with me at all times so that every night I could make a tour of the sites to water them. Because if there was one thing I discovered out in the country, it was that there is time enough for everything.

Life and Times of Michael K, J. M. Coetzee

That all-softening
overpowering knell,

The tocsin of the soul,—
the dinner bell.

~ *Don Juan*, Lord Byron

Coffee: Induces wit.
Good only if it comes
through Havre. After a big
dinner party it is taken standing
up. Take it without sugar—very
swank; gives the impression you
have lived in the East.

~ Dictionnaire des Idèes Reçues,
Gustave Flaubert

Fishiest of all fish places was the
Try Pots, which well deserved its name;
for the pots there were always boiling
chowders. Chowder for breakfast, and chowder for dinner, and chowder for supper, till you
began to look for fish-bones coming through your
clothes. The area before the house was paved with
clam-shells. Mrs. Hussey wore a polished necklace of
codfish vertabrae; and Hosea Hussey had his account
books bound in superior old shark-skin. There was a fish
flavor to the milk too, which I could not at all account for,
till one morning happening to take a stroll along the
beach among some fishermen's boats I saw Hosea's
brindled cow feeding on fish remnants, and marching
along the sand with each foot in a cod's decapitated
head, looking very slipshod, I assure ye.

Moby Dick, Herman Melville

It was the old substantial
dinner you get in a country
hotel and consisted of *vol-au-vent
à la financière,* fowls boiled in rice,
beans with a sauce and vanilla creams,
iced and flavored with burnt sugar.
The ladies made an especial onslaught
on the boiled fowl and rice: their stays
seemed about to burst; they wiped their
lips with slow, luxurious movements.

~ *Nana,* Emile Zola

So she quitted the warm
Belgian house and the vaulted
kitchen that smelled of gas, new
bread and coffee; she left behind the
piano, the violin, the big Salvator Rosa
inherited from her father, the tobacco-jar
and the long, slender clay pipes, the coke
braziers, the open books and crumpled
newspapers, and as a young bride, she
entered the country house isolated during
the hard winters in that forest land.

~ *My Mother's House*, Colette

When questioning aunts and uncles, parents, and grandparents about your family's origins, stories of the old days are bound to appear, laden with comments about how bad the old place and its ways were—or how good. My mother, who spent her childhood in Fort Worth, Texas during the depression, repeatedly told me a story about a pot of beans. Her mother, my grandmother, worked in a slaughterhouse during those years and early every morning before she left for work she would start a pot of beans on the back of the stove. My mother said that when she got up she always felt secure because she knew there would be food to eat that day.

Part of the fun of discovering these origins is doing further research. If you learn that an ancestor came across the Great Plains in the 1850s, read travelers' accounts of the trip, and in doing so you'll learn about the food your ancestor might have eaten, and the rigors, accomplishments, and tragedies of the trip. The stories about your family will then be set in a larger context.

Often family stories are regional, particular to a certain area. Advance research on the region can add depth to your questions. If your family origins are Italian, for example, ask your relatives what region in Italy the family came from. Each region has its own specialties, and they vary greatly from one to another. See if anyone in your family has memories handed down to them of what they ate in the old country, or of how they gathered and prepared the food. One Italian recently told me about relatives who soaked their olives first in mountain streams to get the bitterness out, then in the sea to salt them and give them flavor. After that, they were kept in olive oil seasoned with wild fennel and thyme. Everyone's family origins are filled with such stories.

When I was ten years old, our family made its first trip to the Far East. Even though I had eaten Chinese food my entire life, I had my first taste of the life of an epicure. In those days, Mama had said Chinese food in America was unrefined and, as we dined in Hong Kong, I finally understood what she meant. The dim sum were like jewels, studded with the tiniest pieces of vegetable—like slivers of bamboo shoots, finely minced water chestnuts, shreds of scallions— amazing to look at and more delectable to savor. Morsels so delicate they bore no resemblance to the big, clumsy things we called dim sum in San Francisco. These were works of art. This is what my parents meant when they said, "You must take heart to prepare."

The Wisdom of the Chinese Kitchen, Grace Young

I declare that a meal
prepared by a person who
loves you will do more good
than any average cooking and
on the other side of it a person
who dislikes you is bound to
get that dislike into your food,
without intending to.

~ *The Harvest of Years*,
Luther Burbank

Dis-moi ce que
tu manges, je te
dirai ce que tu es.

Tell me what you eat
and I will tell you
what you are.

~ *Physiologie du Goût,*
    Anthelme Brillat-Savarin

It was now high time for the peasant family to get into the boat, but they would not go before they had, loudly weeping, kissed the hands of their relievers and piled blessings upon them. The old woman insisted upon handing over to them an old stable lantern with a couple of spare tallow candles, a jug of water, and a keg of gin, together with a loaf of the hard black bread which the peasants of the Westerlands make.

"The Deluge at Norderney," *Seven Gothic Tales*, Isak Dinesen

I would eat
my own father
with such a sauce.

~ L'Amanach des Gourmands,
Grimod de la Reynière

The only way to
keep a family in existence
for generations is to think
cabbage-stalks nice.

~ Chinese Proverb

reference books

Counihan, Carole and Penny Van Esterik, eds. *Food and Culture: A Reader.*
Routledge, NJ: Routledge Press, 1997.
A collection of essays by anthropologists, food writers, and cultural theorists. Sometimes dry and academic, but worthwhile for the reader interested in probing into the deeper meanings of food and eating.

Herbst, Sharon Tyler. *The New Food Lover's Companion.* Hauppauge, NY:
Barrons Educational Series, Inc., 1995.

McGee, Harold. *On Food and Cooking: The Science and Lore of the Kitchen.* New York:
Collier Books, 1997.

Ostmann, Barbara Gibbs and Jane L. Baker. *The Recipe Writer's Handbook.*
New York: John Wiley & Sons, 1997.

Stobbart, Tob. *Herbs, Spices, and Flavorings.* New York: Viking, 1986.

Willan, Anne. *La Varenne Practique.* New York: Crown Publishing, 1989.

food memoirs and stories

Beard, James, and James Villaca. *American Taste: A Celebration of Gastronomy Coast-to-Coast.* New York: Lyons Press, 1997.

Bernadin, Tom. *The Ellis Island Immigrant Cookbook: The Story of Our Common Past Told Through the Recipes and Reminiscences of Our Immigrant Ancestors.* New York:
Tom Bernadin Inc., 1994.
This is a wonderful collection of recipes, introduced by personal stories. Many of the recipes were handed down verbally through the generations.

Dinesen, Isak (Karen Blixen). *Anecdotes of Destiny.* New York: Vintage
Books, 1993.
Contains the short story "Babette's Feast," later made into an award-winning film of the same name.

Esquivel, Laura. *Like Water for Chocolate.* New York: Doubleday, 1992.
A wonderful tale of family life and love, interspersed with mysterious recipes such as "Quail and Rose Petal Sauce."

Fisher, M. F. K. *Consider the Oyster.* New York: North Point Press, 1988.
M. F. K. Fisher is the high priestess of the American gastronomical essay, a delicious prose stylist as well as a compiler of early 20th-century recipes and reminiscences.

Fisher, M. F. K. *The Gastronomical Me.* New York: North Point Press, 1989.
Collection of autobiographical essays, each taken from a different period of the author's life and set across the U.S. and Europe. Not to be read on an empty stomach!

Halpern, Daniel, ed. *Not for Bread Alone: Writers on Food, Wine, and the Art of Eating.* Hopewell, NJ: Ecco Press, 1993.
A collection of twenty-two essays by American and European writers ranging from Charles Lamb to Alice Waters and Joyce Carol Oates.

Kamman, Madeleine. *When French Women Cook: A Gastronomic Memoir.* New York: Macmillan, 1996.
A collection of regional French recipes, a personal memoir, and a love letter to the cooks who influenced the life and palate of one of America's greatest cooks and food writers.

Trillin, Calvin. *The Tummy Trilogy: American Fried/Alice, Let's Eat/Third Helpings.* New York: Noonday Press, 1994.
A collection of this humorist's essays from the 1970s and early '80s. Trillin focuses on down-home eatin', the everyday culinary legacy of our American ancestors.

Visser, Margaret. *Much Depends on Dinner: The Extraordinary History and Mythology, Allure and Obsessions, Perils and Taboos of an Ordinary Meal.* New York: Grove Press, 1986.
In nine chapters, each devoted to a particular food such as "Rice: The Tyrant with A Soul" and "Ice Cream: Cold Comfort," Ms. Visser, a classicist, examines the culture, history, and lore of our relationship to food.

——. *The Rituals of Dinner: The Origins, Evolution, Eccentricities, and Meaning of Table Manners.* New York: Penguin Books, 1992.
In chapters such as "Learning to Behave," "Dinner is Served," and "No Offense," all sorts of food habits from a wide variety of cultures are explored in a most amusing way.

Williams, Thelma Howard. *Our Family Table: Recipes and Food Memories from African American Life Models.* Memphis: Tradery House, 1993.

Winegardener, Mark, ed. *We Are What We Ate: 24 Memories of Food.* San Diego: Harcourt Brace & Company, 1998.
A collection of memories of food by some of the United States most recognized writers, such as Paul Auster, Wendell Berry, and Richard Russo.

Young, Grace. *The Wisdom of the Chinese Kitchen: Classic Family Recipes of Celebrations and Healing.* New York: Simon & Schuster, 1999.
A collection of family recipes by a first-generation American, richly and lovingly interspersed with stories of her parents, extended family, and herself in the context of food.